Colors in My World

Red in My World

By Brienna Rossiter

level 1
little blue readers

www.littlebluehousebooks.com

Little Blue House is distributed by North Star Editions:
sales@northstareditions.com | 888-417-0195

Produced for Little Blue House by Red Line Editorial.

Photographs ©: Shutterstock Images, cover, 4, 7, 8–9, 11, 13, 15, 16 (top left), 16 (top right), 16 (bottom left), 16 (bottom right)

Library of Congress Control Number: 2020900834

ISBN
978-1-64619-161-1 (hardcover)
978-1-64619-195-6 (paperback)
978-1-64619-263-2 (ebook pdf)
978-1-64619-229-8 (hosted ebook)

Printed in the United States of America
Mankato, MN
082020

About the Author

Brienna Rossiter enjoys playing music, reading books, and drinking tea. She lives in Minnesota.

Table of Contents

I See Red

The car is red.

The bird is red.

bird

The slide is red.

slide

The ball is red.

The door is red.

The pot is red.

pot

Glossary

ball

door

bird

slide

Index